there can be nothing after this

While every precaution has been taken in the preparation of this book, the publisher assumes no responsibility for errors or omissions, or for damages resulting from the use of the information contained herein.

THERE CAN BE NOTHING AFTER THIS

First edition. July 15, 2024.

ISBN: 979-8227867476

Written by Allen Seward.

With special thanks to:

Big Windows Review for the first publication of *even the TV static sounds like music to us now*,

Oddball Magazine for the first publication of *the burning hours*,

and *A Thin Slice of Anxiety* for the first publication of *brown bottled beer, my poetry, #talkallnight, while listening to Tom Waits, zone of empty,* and *the atheists*

yes, you

how long until we wring
out the clouds

pull the sky down

send it all
into
the crapper?

figuratively, of course

this is not a
literal
world.

not while the pages
all
drip with blood

and not just the poems:

tax returns, and audits,
eviction notices,
parking tickets, speeding tickets,
spreadsheets, customer
reports, criminal histories,
letters home
from war-killed love,
appeals to government,

liability insurance, escrow
accounts, rent,
grocery lists and receipts,
library cards, TV guides
and phone books and
tabloids that still
find reasons to exist,
all of it scabby
and stinking, the
pages all stuck together;

poetry, smut, hardcore
pornography, notes
scrawled on coffee-ringed
napkins, all bloody,
vacation requests, notices
of termination,
polling numbers, ballots,
all covered in bodily
matter,

Xmas cards, fiscal reports,
newsletters, Bible verses,
novels, biographies, treaties,
declarations of war (for
obvious reasons), family
recipes, interviews, FBI
profiles, manifestos,
party invitations, notes to
self, appointment cards,
all smeared in human
juices, some dried, some
fresh, covered in death,
papers and information

outliving us, in
the landfill or kitchen
drawers or aether;

you there

yes, you

how long until it's
done
and done

until the coffin
gets its
last nail

until the powers
that be
press down their
thumbs?

hallelujah,

the doomed

the damned

the fucked

the torn toenail
sunset

the wishing wells

obliterated

the stanza ruined or
just not very good

the personality stripped
of
itself

the jagged teeth
coming down

the sad sloppy state
of
the end.

hallelujah, you say.

you there.
yes, you.

each time you lose a bet, you should wager double on the next match

the dead come out to play, to smile,

alligator teeth and
rabbit tears,

we place the wrong bets but we don't care.

no.

we knew we were going to lose,

it's fine.

Luck be with you, but Luck
does not
smile,
Luck does not think,
Luck does not
care. no.

we were born into this boat, this same
boat,

that's a fact.

no one likes to admit it, but that's the truth.

that's Luck.

the dead come out to play,
and that's
Luck.

alligator teeth and
rabbit tears,
and
that's Luck.

the mailman blowing a tire,
and that's Luck.

oh yea,
it's all bad, all boring.
disco's dead
and Jesus puts cigarettes
out on his chest.

how's that for being saved?

heeding the ocean's call
with hot teeth in your vein.
I doubt you rushed your existence,
letting waves carry you,
knowing demons who would only share
chameleon current and colored wind.
creamy sunsets take you
as you admire the steady night.
you are called back to your wet time.
you were a sad man, weren't you?

this seed was planted in
my
stomach
it sprouted and began to grow
up through my body
and into my throat
until the flower bloomed in my mouth

roots in my stomach

thorns in my neck

rose petals for teeth

I am in bloom.

it's the running joke
of this life
that I should come here
to this place
again again and again
to earn my existence
to
not die

that I should sit here
inside this thing
at the top of my neck
and of all things smile

that I should look to
some rich and famous person
so I might be
lifted up

or that I
should sit at the feet of
some philosopher
so I might understand
myself
that I might know
how to live

that we are all compelled
to do this, to be
this
there is no way out

but there is
always hope
hope tied to the
finger of another

the punchline is deafening
and if you don't laugh
then you're just too dumb
to get it
it was all written
by the greatest comic
in the world
after all

but you there
sitting inside your own
hollowed-out sockets
your arms thin and
branch-like
you get it, too
I can see

you're on the track to
being
a bigass winner
just like the rest
of us

it's your own fault
for falling so low

grace came for you
but you were otherwise
engaged

that's it, isn't it?

even if we are afforded
the opportunity
to assimilate
we are not afforded
the chance to rise up
just a little

no,

the hierarchy will strike you
down

you will be kissed
dead and cold

it's the running joke
of this life
that things are the
way they are
and we're all here

that this is it

our big chance

but the shot was missed
at birth

it's enough to make
the brain eat itself

it's enough to make
the soul walk out the door

just cut your teeth
on tomorrow
until tomorrow doesn't come

oh yes,

isn't it something?

all the agony
all the sorryness
all the waiting,

it will finish
eating us
one day and we
will be glad.

if you want to try a new recipe the first thing you must do
is read the advertisements, be invaded, and
just as you scroll through the belly of the text
and find the measurements you must watch a small video,
or try to close a small video. invaded again.

the news does it too: the end of the world punctuated by popups and ad breaks.
I know the Bible is not real because
it does not mention Jesus being sponsored by Nabisco, or
Wonder Bread, or whoever. the Second Coming
does not hinge on us drinking Red Bull,
so we can put a pin in the lake of fire.

pretty soon I won't be able to scratch my balls
without first watching at least fifteen seconds
of an at-home STD test advertisement,
and I won't be able to masturbate without
being alerted of the hot single moms in my area.
I won't be able to kiss my partner
without hearing about some true-crime documentary
detailing how she may-or-will murder me.

one day, years on, I will go to lay flowers
at my mother's grave but before I do
I will hear of the importance of mental health
and for whatever price-per-month
I will be able to chat with a licensed professional
about the flowers I'm trying to lay on my mother's grave.

invaded again.

raw
expression,
words that bite
the way they should.
a prayer
with teeth,
an answer to
an answer.
speech is just a way
to get through
the dark
without groping
for what's not there.
conversation
is just the same
for
the strangest kind
of silence.

and day and night they do not cease

somewhere the angels use their harps
to bash the remaining fish coming ashore.
this didn't go so well last time.
one of us slipped through their ranks and
grew into an ugly desecration.
now we have soap operas, 24/7 news,
DMV's, supermarkets, political rallies,
same-day shipping, alcoholism, Sunday school,
countries, nationalism, genocide, car inspections,
utilities, starvation, no hope, so-called freedom...
I don't blame the angels for wanting to
do away with us. and perhaps,
in some way, we're still doing god's work:
uninhabitable land means no more us,
dried up oceans means no more fish.

A comes first:
first to serve, to be served,
and to die

A takes so much speech

yes, remember this,
remember this hallowed father
of sound
and knowledge
honor words such as *"Alpha"*
and pray only to them—
be careful
when you are drinking
lest you slur their bodies,
poison the well,
and anger your spoken god.

it's a rainy night
so I must write about the rain
because I am—or must be—in tune with Nature,
with Existence,

and so the rain falls...

it is not so easy as drawing a line
lines bend into circles, break in two
become symbols and letters
everything I have ever written was once
part of
some great line, or large box
some shape
and I picked at it as best I could
with my chewed-down fingernails
splinters and flakes came off, finally
something broke free
parts went under the refrigerator, the oven
the couch, the table
rats scurried away
with little objects I had thought
were too heavy to move
I watched them dart into the shadows
back into the walls
where they would conspire with their small treasures
and I would feel light
and dumb
for an hour or two before going to bed
and in the morning were geometries
I had never seen before
I had never thought existed, all floating
in
the air
some making music
and some sounding like tigers
so I had coffee with them
bacon and eggs
I rinsed the dishes and left them in the sink

to wash later
wondering what would break apart
next, what it would look and smell like
how it would sound
and what would be left over.
this was all a natural progression, I think
like the pear tree out back
bearing pears
or not bearing pears, the squirrels coming
to steal fruit off the branches
the sound of one smacking a metal roof
the thud of one hitting the ground
the mail entering the mailbox
the credit card payment coming due
simple wasted time and flesh
foaming ideologues
24hr news, hair trimmings, placebo calm
new age gutters, the internet burning down
Jesus wearing a leather jacket
and smoking a cigarette outside the
new library of Alexandria
all of it made of something else
and looking like oxidized meat.

while you were singing about blackbirds
I was dancing with bluebirds and greenbirds
and red ones and yellow and orange and gray...
they poured me my wine
and we drank together in the yard,
in the sun, and you were huddled
in the corner of some dusty room with nothing
but an ear to the speaker and a voice to the air.

we work and fight and claw
our way through it.
we look for something, anything,
to dull the ache.
we want out of it but
on our own terms.
we would like to, just once,
twist something into shape.

this is the burden of our
existence.
this is what goes on
inside closed skulls.

even now we are amazed
at how much blood we have left.
even now we know
that the dark is supposed to be cold.

so I sip at a beer
and contemplate all things,
and then I do what
none of my forebears had thought of
or were capable of:

I cease my contemplation and just drink my beer.

even the TV static sounds like music to us now

the earth is in ruin
and my hair falls out.

good god, the line is so long!

the air smells like hot breath
and everywhere around me,
wherever I look, is just flesh flesh flesh.

we've turned a corner,

we've put a brick on the gas,

we've juiced the last dinosaur
and something is next.

we turn our eyes
toward a worried face
with
murderous intent.

"you there! yes! you!!"

they run. we run after.

this soup has all become slop,
and it's no wonder no one
wants to taste it.

eat from my ribcage. drink from my wrist.

good god,
we've been at this for what seems
like
forever!

even the TV static sounds like music
to us now!

~Big Windows Review, May 2023

lightning came out my pores
and steam from my mouth
and my mother called a number that was no longer in service.

I will buy this useless crap
and put it
on a shelf
or in a box
where it will pop like beetles
in
the microwave,

and I will never look at it again.

I guess it's only fitting
to write
this poem using a computer
I stole from work

and
print it out using one of the reams
of paper
I stole from work

considering all they've stolen from me
I don't mind the prospect of
damnation
for my sins,
I don't mind the number
being called up or
the
price being paid

I'll take the doors and
hinges
from the place, too,
if I think I can
use
them

it all
exists for a reason,

I
exist for a reason

none of us shall be repaired
yet
none of us shall die.

this is a bad place. shit stinks.
no way out.
no bright morning or happy ending.
I see gummed-up machinery behind your eyes.
it no longer ticks.
nothing makes a sound but pain.
the gods come by every now and then
to ash their cigarettes.
this is a bad place.
water tastes like sad evenings. shit stinks.

my cat has to take a pill
every
other day.

he has asthma.

his first asthma attack almost
killed him,
and
when we found out
what was going on
the
vet told us
that his lungs looked just as bad
as the lungs of
a
cat she had just seen
that was dying
of cancer.

there was almost nothing but
clouds,
smudges, maybe,

nothing that belongs in
the
lungs.

so he needs the pill until
he dies.

I hide it in his
food
and he eats it
and now many days you can't
tell
that he almost died
on the way
to
the emergency
vet.

I
think it's fine
if you
call it something
close
to a
miracle.

the burning hours

the tank is empty
just running on fumes
the metal is soft
as flesh

one day it sputs out
goes nowhere
no more
and the phone rings
but goes unanswered
it sits on the table
and screams

no one is home

even the messages crinkle
and break apart
and flake away

much better, I think,
than going back *there*

much better than these
gross alternatives

I think I will finally sleep
without setting an alarm
and see what's on the other side.

~Oddball Magazine, March 2023

thy hard blue skin, trembling in
trembling hands...thy body tired, worn,
frayed spine and pages yellowing like
smoker's teeth.
'scatter thy pearls upon our love-sick
land that mourns for thee' Blake,
readily decayed by now...
as I will surely be after such time...
your body is whole, your body lives on,
I hold it in my hand.

oh, how it ends...
oh, how they all leave...but I stay, and
I don't know why. no one wants to live here
in this happy place, because it is not a happy place.
there is nothing to it other than what
you see, and what you see is not very good...
at least some of us won't die here, or drink
here at the end of days.
at least some will escape to maybe
be sad and lonely elsewhere when the
dust ignites.

still, I thought I had not-so-very much left
to kill, yet here I am;
some of these bastards are
beating me to the punch, and I am the joke again.
goodbye, you lovely fuckers.
some of you are quite ugly and stupid,
and others have been good to know;
I don't care, though,
good or bad, because you've made it
out and left me behind to torture
the new souls, or be tortured by them.

onward, then,
to other pale horizons, other stagnant waters,
other stale and moldy places. live long and prosper,
or die of alcoholism, cry into the mouth of prognosis.
the world has not yet welcomed you,
and it likely never will. onward, then, to long,
steady looks at other walls—not
here—and new depressions, new rage...new,

but maybe not better; new, but not worse.

you have pissed all over this hell for long enough.
you have earned your rest...and
if not rest, then seven tails instead of nine.

selah.

I
walked in
and played the
first slots I
saw

I was up $20
or so
in no time

I think I went
up to $30

we were still going to
be there another
hour
maybe two

so I
kept at the slots
and watched
my winnings shave off

down
down
down
it went

I was $10 or $12
up now

I was heading
toward even
toward zero

I left the machine
and went to the
bar
got a drink

left it all
as
a tip for the
bartender

left it to the
black leather and
fishnets
the eyes that said

"I know the game"

I think we all do
deep down
somewhere
down
at
that core
it's not so hard
to parse:

a good person would
have just walked
in
the door

handed you the cash
and
left

just like that

but no
sometimes we
piss it all away
instead.

I keep thinking that someone needs to
come to me,
someone needs to pull me up, out,
someone needs to stop me.

this is no way to be.

but here I am.

what's the alternative?

every day that passes is a nail
in a coffin I can't see.
I want to choose some of the nails.
I don't think that's wrong.

as far as we know
we never see our own coffins,
or know what happens to our bodies
after the fact.

it is what it is.

time passes.

tears dry.

all this
and you want me to
hammer the box with overtime?

you want me to care
about productivity?

productivity going nowhere?

my throat is a chimney
I sit by the tracks
and look at the rusted metal
on the cars
the night is soggy
my breath clings to the air
as if refusing to go in peace.

is
that we keep cracking eggs
'til you all stop whining.

omelets be damned,

we just really like
the sound
and the funny snot feel.

a jukebox turns to Bruce Springsteen

ah yes
god slacks his jaw
loose pages are thrown about by an open window
someone, somewhere, robs a bank or
tries to
as a painting dries somewhere else
and someone else reads
about the crucifixion for the very first time
and a jukebox turns to
Bruce Springsteen,
the world cut open on
its own edge
and half of us are fast asleep
and do not notice

William Blake burns a Christmas tree

Napoleon spills a drink

Herodotus
takes the stand to testify.

it seems a worm
has caught the hook
and pulled it
down the fish's mouth

and here we are

not again

here we are

yet again

give the line a tug
as dusk breaks
the water

see what comes up

see what comes up.

I had a nice buzz
going
before you came along
and told me
what the world was.

sounds like a
squall
tastes of stomach acid
and feels like
terminal cancer,

it looks like July-stewed
roadkill

and still I hold it to
my heart
breathing in the stench
of feet, of bleach
of
popped stomach
and burnt hair,

I nuzzle it with my chin

and think of it even as
it does not bother
to even disregard me.

brown bottled beer

the rain starts to come down outside
and I look out the window
as I grab my brown bottled beer
and find that the bottle is empty.

I'll need another.

that's just the way it goes,
isn't it?

if you want to take this
for what it is
then it's nothing, or
nearly nothing.

the clouds are nothing.

the rain is nothing.

but as the rain starts to come down
outside, I look out the window
and reach for my brown bottled beer
and find that the bottle is empty.

I'll need another.

~A Thin Slice of Anxiety, May 2023

the poems are getting shorter.

the short fiction is getting shorter.

the minds are getting shorter, too,
maybe...

if we were not technological beasts
a few years ago, ten years ago maybe,
then we are now...

word limits, line limits,
I don't want to write an epic
but I'd like a page or two, or three.

I suppose I can't blame them though:

I don't think I'd want to read
two or three or more pages
of my poetry either.

~A Thin Slice of Anxiety, May 2023

everyone wants to talk
or no one wants to

talk too much,
talk too loud,
say nothing at all

talk to gods and saints
talk to lovers
talk to ourselves

say what you want
to the other end of
the phone

but we are not in
conversation,
not really

we enjoy the sounds
of meaning
much more
than we enjoy
the meaning itself

everyone wants to talk
and we've forgotten
what silence is really
like, the tinnitus
doesn't help

and on it goes like this
until it doesn't go on
anymore, one day
preferably far off,
at all times
far off

we'll wake up in the dark
of the next life,
hear nothing,
and start to scream.

~A Thin Slice of Anxiety, May 2023

words cut the stone
and
the children all grab
their knives

blood blood blood, out out out,

trees worry out the sunlight
waiting for
a
rain

but rain won't come for
three-
or-
four days.

the wind blows. it's chill.

the TV's
there
talking in the other room

a draft
comes in through
one
of the windows

I look out the window
and
see a brood of

those children
swinging their knives in
the
white sunlight
all of them wearing
red
shirts by now

and they're coming
my
way.

~*A Thin Slice of Anxiety, May 2023*

for all your visits to the dentist
and all the gold
in your mouth,

how could your smile be so cheap?

you have entered a zone
of
empty

and found that you like the way
it makes your voice sound,

you like the look of being
the tallest
person there,

and the only voice, too.

now to find something
to
prop your
foot on...

~*A Thin Slice of Anxiety, May 2023*

there are no atheists
in
foxholes,

smugly
say
those who
cry

catch for us the foxes!
the little foxes!

the foxes must
be
put to death
for the
sake of
our
wine!

catch for us the poets,
they should
say,

for we will drain
your
vineyards dry.

~A Thin Slice of Anxiety, May 2023

I would like to put into
perspective
how very much I
miss
you:

here is a picture I drew
of
a fish
in the third grade.

incognito
in the dark
no one home
no one watches
no one listens
even the walls look away

the end of all things will not be televised

doom is open and the prices are listed
out front.

this is not some cheap thing,
but it is permanent.

don't be fooled by knockoff fates
and demises:
they can be set like broken bones, repaired,
they can be healed improperly but
still healed.

reality is up for grabs and the takers
are all sad
because one day it will all be picked clean
and there won't be enough left to go around
let alone keep to yourself.

put your money down. take out a second mortgage.
start a betting pool.

the lips of heady monsters wait to be kissed.

About the Author

Allen Seward is a poet from the Eastern Panhandle of West Virginia. His work has appeared in Scapegoat Review, DEDpoetry, JAKE, miniMAG, Skyway Journal, The Charleston Anvil, and The Big Windows Review, among others. He currently resides in WV with his partner and four cats.

@AllenSeward1 on Twitter (currently known as "X")

@allenseward0 on Instagram

xoxo

Read more at https://wordpress.com/view/allenseward.wordpress.com.